If You Must Fall Bush

Nsah Mala

Langaa Research & Publishing CIG
Mankon, Bamenda

Publisher:
Langaa RPCIG
Langaa Research & Publishing Common Initiative Group
P.O. Box 902 Mankon
Bamenda
North West Region
Cameroon
Langaagrp@gmail.com
www.langaa-rpcig.net

Distributed in and outside N. America by African Books Collective
orders@africanbookscollective.com
www.africanbookscollective.com

ISBN: 9956-763-85-3

© Nsah Mala 2016

DISCLAIMER
All views expressed in this publication are those of the author and do not
necessarily reflect the views of Langaa RPCIG.

Table of Contents

Preface

If You Must Fall Bush is a collection of highly figurative poems by Kenneth Toah Nsah, alias Nsah Mala, a young poet who has stamped his footprints on the poetry scene with the publication of his much acclaimed *Bites of Insanity* and *Chaining Freedom*. Composed mostly in the first half of 2015, the poems in this new collection resonate with the same verve and imagistic intensity and stylistic experimentation characteristic of Nsah Mala's poetic oeuvre. Poems included in this eclectic collection cover a wide gamut of thematic and aesthetic forms spanning across panegyrics, acrostics, satires, elegies, eulogies, indictments, etc.

As a matter of fact, this collection of poems can be referred to as the poetry of everyday life. In other words, the poet does not set out primarily to engage in abstractions or to contemplate the purely metaphysical universe, but rather to take stock of the facts, realities, signs, sounds and sights around him that produce, shape and condition his existence and his place in the world. That notwithstanding, the realities that the poet describes, decries and denounces are a result of complex and entangling historical processes, both local and global, economic and political, that have conjured to produce his socio-political situation. The poems thus take stock of his being in the society, in a particular location or at the intersection of specific spaces, for instance, in the case of poems on migration. The poet uses his lived experience as primary material for his poetic imagination and from this basis, proceeds to weave themes and situations that address pertinent issues in his society. In short, Nsah Mala's poetry emerges from a very specific space of locution, hence its subjectivity, characteristic of every poetic imagination, marked in most of the poems by an enunciatory "I". This "I" is however not born out of egotism or solipsistic mindset, but rather it is a socialised or shared subjectivity given that what occurs to this "I" is rather symptomatic of the general situation in which several other compatriots are entrapped. Thus, even though subjective, Nsah Mala's poetic voice captures experiences that resonate wide beyond the poetic persona cum author, making this a highly committing and engaging collection.

The pertinence of the subject of locution comes out clearly in the tribute poems that the poet dedicates to specific figures ranging from academics, lawyers, politicians, etc some of whom have been and continue to be of prime inspiration to the poet and his fellow compatriots. These poems intimate the fact that beyond the quasi-general decline in values, professional ethics and ethical conscience, there are still some exemplary figures that stand up as models worth emulating. In an inverse current that steers away from the invectives levied against venal political figures are lambasted, Nsah Mala acclaims and celebrates the lives of these epitomes of virtue, some of who are deceased. On the latter note, the poet portrays the unpredictability, transience and ephemerality of human life exposed to the arbitrary verdict of (what Hardy refers to as) Crass Casualty. The poet's elegy exudes heart-rending currents of agony in the poems "Innocent Martyrs" and "Roasted Martyrs" written in memory of "Little Favour Nsani and Other Victims of the Bamungo-Oku Road Accident of Saturday 22 December 2013" on their way to celebrate the Christmas in their hometown. These elegiac poems underline the metaphysical dimension of Nsah Mala's poetry, the mystery of life or being. In such elegies and other poems of political indictment, the poet evokes the existence of a Supreme Being capable of carrying out some form of poetic justice and divine judgment. The validity and credibility of such belief depends on the subjectivity of each and every reader.

Beyond the sharp categories of panegyric and indictment, it is however important to note that some of Nsah Mala's poems are rather ambiguous in tonality, reuniting both praise and indictment in the same poem. Thus the poem indicts as it praises, debases as it glorifies, a characteristic aspect of Malinkegriot, a court poet/historian who infuses his praise with irony, undermining the legitimacy of the King when the latter engages in unscrupulous practices. The "Eulogy to Foyn B" turns out to be a proper indictment, parodying the whole notion of eulogy itself. In "To the Soldiers up North", while extolling the prowess and the exemplary valor of the soldiers combating the lethal lunatics of Boko Haram in the Northern part of the country, the poem concurrently denounces the putative Commander-in-Chief of the National Armed Forces for his governance by proxy and failure to pay deserved tribute to the fallen soldiers. Even if one were to accept the illegitimate title conferred on Foyn B as the Foyn of Foyns, his negligence, lack of responsibility and indifference can only earn him contempt from his "subjects".

This brings us to the nature of the relation between literary creativity and socio-political discourse. Literary discourse is a discourse that comes after all other discourses based on assertive truths, positivistic affirmations and revolutionary fervor have made their pompous procession to the social "stage". In the face of a rather Foucauldian fabrication of the subject through political discourse, literary discourse constitutes an interventionist discourse that interjects, intercepts, interpolates and exposes the vacuity of such political slogans and buzzwords that flourish in the postcolonial public sphere. In reality, postcolony is the era of the rule of discourses/speeches which in effect bear absolutely no proximity with the lived experiences of the citizens which they claim to invoke and represent. Ultimately, language plays the rule of concealing reality instead of expressing it. Who can believe slogans like "emerging economy by 2035", "motion of support", "development", "digitalization", beyond the fact that they are meant to serve the political expediency of a particular regime at a specific point in time? The derision of such terminology in poems like "My Motion of Support", "When I go to the Public Service", "Fallen Tree at the Public Service", show the disenchantment with a political system prone to pre-bendalism, rent-seeking and neo-patrimonialism, while the endless monologue of the State continues to sustain the fiction of unity, progress, unity, peace, fatherland. The question thus is: has not politics become more fictional than a work of art?

The eponymous poem, *If You Must fall Bush* and others on the thematics of migration to the West and emerging economies of the East, grants insights into a complex hegemonic configuration of global political economy and (what the Argentine critic Walter Mignolo refers to as) the geopolitics of knowledge. The global politics of knowledge and the configuration of the global economic situation predispose youths from the Global South to consistently dream of furthering their education in Western and some of the Eastern countries. In many cases, the prior cause for this migration lies in the socio-political and economic situation of the home country. The dream of a better study and (most importantly) economic environment is often nurtured without proper calculation of the aggregate risks/opportunities involved. Thus, when such dreams are deferred in the host countries, some of which are not much better in many aspects than home country, the outcome is frustration, depression, disillusionment, alienation, nostalgia, and, in extreme cases, suicide.

The government of the home country shares the responsibility of this dire situation for not investing adequately in educational infrastructure and for not inscribing studies abroad within a strategic national development policy. The result in most cases is brain drain, academic slavery, and epistemological hegemony, instead of a win-win situation of brain exchange or what is known in recent vocabulary of funding institutions as *brain circulation*. This geopolitics of knowledge bears striking affinity with colonialist paradigms which inscribe the Global South as sempiternal reserves of raw materials, intellectual deficiency and cultural retardation, needing the redemptive hand of the West and the East. This situation, when amplified by the orientalist images churned out by certain jaundiced Western media outlets, completely discounts non-Western countries as equally worthwhile poles of knowledge production and competencies to reckon with.

Thus, a key aspect of this poetry collection, equally characteristic of other works of the author, especially *Do you Know Mbesa?*, is the belief that access and appurtenance to the so-called global cultures can only be done through the valorization of our "local" cultures. This is seen through his rich pool of culture-specific imagery and the infusion of a sense of locale in his poems as he seeks to illuminate universal and foreign experiences through local imagery and vernacular patterns of expression. In relation to poems on his *bushfalling* experience, the author stresses the aggregate potentials and strengths of home universities in relation to their Western counterparts, positing that educational systems in the world need to coexist in a context of interdependence and corporation.

Reading through the poems, one might be tempted to think that the author is quite pessimistic about life abroad. However, the poems rather constitute a critique of the false and unbridled expectations, illusions, shortsightedness and naiveté that sometimes characterize the desires of students from developing countries to emigrate to the Global North with ambitions of quick and instant success. As such, his personal *faux pas* does not in any way signify failure of his life's ambitions but rather an instigation to reconsider and re-think his prior rationale for emigration. The abortive attempt to foster education abroad is re-tailored unto a learning and, most importantly, creative process. Beyond a mere therapeutic effect, the author's unrealized journey motif saves as an eye-opener for him to better appreciate the geo-political realities of the world. The homebound *bushfaller* learns from his experiences and thus nurtures a fervent desire to assume his responsibilities in nation-building and if need be only emigrate on carefully thought out motif. Through this experience, the poet becomes wiser, seizing the "opportunity" to re-constitute the self, re-assess his life objectives and to conscientiously strive towards a dignified achievement.

As a point of conclusion, a keen interest deserves to be accorded to the poet's self-reflexivity with regard to the creative process. He leads us into the crevices of his creative process, revealing the circumstances that led to the crafting of specific poems, detailing the trajectories of the drafts and the modifications they have undergone to attain their present stage. These forms of para-texts can constitute an interesting element of study in contemporary *internet studies* that focus on the intricate relationship between cyber- technology and modes of creative writing, the evolving connotation of "manuscripts" in the post-modern cyber age, hypertextuality, etc. In effect, the creative process is thus painted as the result of human effort, produced in real-life circumstances in a techno-savvy age. Beyond any transcendental and mystifying accounts of the creative process characteristic of classical poetry, the poetic inspiration is born out of human effort to express his perspective on social realities and the human condition. As any conscious human effort, poetic vision, far from being etched in stone, is subject to re-visions, re-writing, re-making and always in a process of becoming.

Gilbert Ndi Shang, PhD
University of Bayreuth, 2015

Foreword

Literature is said to be the higher form of language and poetry is the sublime expression of this truth. Poetry's uniqueness lies partly in its double-edged capacity to load a few words with depth of meaning(s) when compared to prose, for example. The poet's capacity to craft, transmit and educe some of the deepest emotions expressible in language always captures and conveys especially esoteric truths that only the few who have drunk of Pegasus's fountain can articulate. Nsah Mala in *If You Must Fall Bush* has proven himself to be one of such beautiful minds whose poetry strongly articulates the necessity for hard work, believe in mother Africa as well as the denigration of hypocrites and sellouts.

Although the collection's title refers to the migration mania popularly known as *bushfalling* in Cameroon, Mala moves beyond that to explore issues like literary production and publishing, nationalism, corruption, lament on the erosion of culture, homage to role models and the military as well as eulogies. These diverse themes come together to make the collection refreshing and interesting to different people for different reasons.

Mala as a writer sets off by paying homage to the art of writing and writers because writers, according to him, are consistently producing new fruits. They are forever fertile in the works that they consistently produce but unfortunately Cameroonian authors have a problem because they do not have publication channels. In most cases their works take so much time to be published so much so that they are accused of plagiarism which the poet creatively terms the accusation of "adultery and fornication". Those involved in publishing in

Cameroon only care about producing textbooks for the syllabus thereby marginalising creative writers. This sense of frustration which Mala expresses is a sentiment that other Cameroonian writers like Joyce Ashuntantang and Oscar Labang have also explored.

Decrying corruption is also a major preoccupation of the poet in this collection and he portrays a situation in which people act without morals. A country that plans to emerge by 2035 should have a blueprint of that emergence plan and do concrete work that will lead to that aim. Unfortunately, the system is corrupt and decaying as evident in poems like "When I Go to Public Service" and "World Market of Diseases". These poems are filled with disappointment expressed through the use of satire and anaphora. The situation at public service where civil servants go to follow up their documents is appalling; there is never any progress and no place to find reliable information or even seat down. Ironically, people write motions of support to the corrupt government. Another disgusting scene is the hospital system that the poet describes as the world market of diseases where people rather pick up diseases like AIDS and cholera instead of being cured. There is the sentiment of disgust as the poet invites the reader, "Let's go to CHU... the world market of diseases... a place where patients cure doctors". This goes to show that there is a problem that is essentially brought about by corruption. Yet there seems to be some hope as the poet praises role models like Barrister Forcheh Edward who is the "messiah of the law profession" and the hope for change in his "jobless Eldorado and corrupt fatherland".

The poet is an individual attached to his culture and uses his poetry to show how modernism has eroded a beautiful culture. He dwells on issues like communalism, an aspect that

Africa is much appreciated for. Yet he paints a picture of human selfishness in which individualism has created new, fake nuclear families instead of the extended families in which people have "countless mothers and brothers and sisters". Another beautiful cultural element that has been erased by modernism is the art of storytelling which was educational since it was a means through which people learnt about their culture. Today, the flat screen TVs, computers and cell phones have replaced this cultural learning process.

The migration syndrome is explored at length ranging from the xenophobic attacks in South Africa wherein Nelson Mandela's legacy is blemished when nationals of some of the countries that hosted ANC exiled members during the apartheid era are maltreated. It is sad that such hard work and effort should be sabotaged by ignorant or short-memory individuals.

Sadly too, slavery is still a lived reality in our 21st century world as Nsah Mala graphically depicts the suffering meted out to Africans in Lebanon, Kuwait and other countries. But the focus is not so much on the perpetrators as on the victims. It is totally incredulous that people could be so gullible as to subject themselves to slavery. The ironic "flight to slavery" in which people sacrifice their dignities for a life of hard labour and cruelty ends with nothing to show for it except perhaps their return home with the physical and emotional scars of their self-willed abused. Although awareness is raised daily on the issue of human trafficking and slavery, people still follow the dreams of greener pastures only to regret when it's too late.

The poet recounts personal experiences in Turkey as he goes there on a scholarship yet he misses Cameroon so much especially the food. Although Istanbul is such a beautiful city, he would rather be in Cameroon. While his scholarship offer letter promises a Master's degree with a thesis, his Turkish host university starts imposing a non-thesis Master's on him upon his arrival: "Baited with a master's thesis offer//Into a salty academic sea with no thesis-plankton". He insists therefore that if one must go abroad, it is important to go with some dignity. To him it is not necessary to go to study the same courses that African universities already offer. He thus calls himself a runner-away bushfaller.

To travel abroad becomes bad when people follow illegal routes and become transformed "into raw material" chartered away in cargo vessels. Furthermore, there is no need to "sell family property" as is often the case with many people since "you need them when you return like a prodigal son" There is so much potential in the homeland and there is really no reason to "go from bush to bush like a rabbit".

The poetic versatility, the broad spectrum of reality and human experiences of the author are reflected in the poet's variety in theme and tone. His capacity to convey and elicit emotions gives the collection the buoyancy of a page-turner. There is no doubt that the poet is nostalgic for the truly human. That he is not at home with lots about his world cuts across the collection. And this is only one of the dimensions that give the collection a sense of unity. In all, Nsah Mala is a young poet who is coming into his own; who is critical of the status quo; the stupidity of wanderlust and the need to reinstate positive natural and cultural values and, yes, communal human values. *If You Must Fall Bush* is a must-read.

Professor Father Michael Suh Niba, PhD
Vice Chancellor, Catholic University of Bamenda,
2015

Reviews

In a caustic tone and satirical humour, Nsah Mala once more considers the ills that plague our society as was the case in his first two collections. Yet this time around, his style is more complex and the imagery depicted is overwhelmingly repugnant. His verses evoke a society adrift: prey to the ravages of the selfish and irresponsible actions of modern man or, better still, postmodern man. Escape does not seem to be possible, not even in foreign climes. The destruction heralded is predictably taking eschatological proportions! Is salvation envisageable?

Yvonne Iden NGWA, PhD
Lecturer, ENS Yaoundé, 2015

If You Must Fall Bush offers an unambiguous cautionary statement on the multitudinous and multifaceted hot-button politico-socio-economic issues confronting and degrading the African continent. In this collection of fifty four poems, Nsah Mala, as if reminding us of the popular saying that "a fool at forty is a fool forever", generously and whole-heartedly eulogises scintillating and hope-instilling examples of personal sacrifices, loyalty and good role-modeling that have brought honour and fame to the continent while bitterly but edifyingly castigating gruesome and ubiquitous instances of bribery and corruption, inhuman political manipulations and oppression, and wanton economic exploitation and subjugation that drive the myopic "bush-falling" (greener-

pasture-searching)   tendencies   and   fantasies
that characterise the youth and future leaders of our time.

Ekpe Inyang
Environmentalist, Playwright & Poet, 2015
(2014 Winner of Eko Prize for Emerging Anglophone
Writers)

Crafting a book is as important as taking it to the readers.

Literary (Re)Production

Literary (re)production is like childbirth.
It is childbirth without restrictive family planning.
No fixed gestation periods in this childbirth.
Only author-parents choose their birth spacing.

Good literary parents are excellent guinea pigs
Who conceive as soon as delivery takes place.
But they cannot eat their babies like hungry pigs
No matter the thorns and famines in their place.

Fertile author-parents also sleep eternally giving life
Because throughout life they are carrying pregnancies.
When they prematurely or maturely reach the exit of life,
They then wish the world goodbye still with pregnancies...

(Mbankolo, 28 March 2015)

Publishing Conundrum

Bites of Inanity's birth certificate
Was signed at Langaa maternity
On February 12, 2015;
But her father only embraced the baby
At home on April 28, 2015,
After a long, long "on attend l'enfant".

How long shall this continue?
That we conceive children in Cameroon
And cannot be delivered in local maternities.
Where are our Cameroonian literary midwives?
Perhaps Ashuntantang's call fell on stone ears;
We keep owning foreign children conceived here.

Our land is blessed with literary fertility,
But sometimes our pregnancies are overdue
And someone elsewhere begets a child similar to ours.
Then we are accused of literary fornication and adultery.
Our midwives chase shadows of textbooks and booklists
While foreigners name our kids and decide their shapes...

How long shall these publishing conundrum continue?

(Mbankolo, Ascension Thursday, 14 May 2015)

No writer is alone since no man is an island.

No New Madiba?

(Following recent xenophobic attacks in S.A.)

Madiba fought fearlessly,
Like David against Goliath,
To end the atrocities of Apartheid.
He closed gushing taps of black blood
And sealed them off with the balm of love.
Madiba gave his entire life,
Like Christ did at Golgotha,
In the struggle to bring peace and fraternity...
He sprinkled dusts of love and forgiveness
On all stagnant lakes and rivers of black blood.

Madiba washed the feet of South Africans,
Like Jesus washed the feet of apostles,
Irrespective of blackness or whiteness.
He swept the broken and burnt black bodies
With the brooms of brotherliness and sisterliness.

But after his peaceful ascension into the angelic realm,
Ingrates and modern brutes have soiled and stained
Madiba's prison-earned achievements and legacies.
They now open fountains of foreign black & white blood;
They now provoke waterfalls of endless innocent blood.

Madiba synergised with foreign brothers and sisters
To earn peace, love and freedom in South Africa;
But soon after his merited departure, xenophobic savages
Are lynching and slaughtering these brothers and sisters.

Human intestines out in broad daylight?
No new Madiba?

(Mbankolo, Ascension Thursday 14 May 2015)

Charles Ngiewih Teke

Committed and creative critic
Highly grounded in literary criticism
Available whenever I call in want
Reviews insightfully and constructively
Lighting flames of creativity in me
Encouraging younger ones to grow and
Supervising them meticulously

No-nonsense professor and
Godfather full of commitment
Identifier of my poetry endowments
Evaluator of my creative pursuits
Wonderful mentor of all ages
Inspirer of my academic visions
Highly-acclaimed literary researcher

Truth's apostle within and without
Emblem of hard work and optimism
Kind son, husband, father, brother, friend
Eager for celestial and terrestrial achievements

(Mbankolo, 28 March 2015)

For Barrister Forcheh Edward

Barrister Forcheh, I salute your example!
Messiah of the Law Profession in rotten Cameroon!
Who could dream a trustworthy & humble lawyer in this
Hell?

Countless young Cameroonians who love Law
Usually end up in brain-drain labs in the Diaspora.
For them, and for me, Law in Rio Dos Cameros is a visa to
Hell:
It's built on falsehood, bribery, unending quest for cling-
cling-cling…

But like Shakespeare of Literature and Newton of Chemistry,
You and Ntumfor Halle have planted new seeds of Law,
Founding your Law career on truth, generosity, kindness,
mercy…
You have said NO to the money-baited hooks of evil.
Your colleagues, raised on soils of inhuman law practices,
Pay you in coins & bank notes of accusations and insults!
Open confrontation and at times isolation have not been left
out.
Yet, we scanty good Cameroonians owe you gross debts of
thanks.

In Ndop and Limbe where you worked,
You even sponsored driving licenses and other documents
(Things you are supposed to jail people for not possessing!)
For some poor miserable persons in this jobless Eldorado.

So you deleted a huge segment of the poverty line dividing
Bald-headed, pot-bellied Rich and
Pale-looking, sunken-eyes, and bony Poor.
 O my corrupt Fatherland!
Suppose you only had five of such children!
The Malachi of misery of this Limbo will come in a single
day.

My mind forever knows where and when I first met you,
Forcheh.
It was a fateful Saturday, 12 January 2008.
ENSAB Bambili was raining some drops of tutors
Onto our jobless Kingdom.
It is probable that you had a close one among these few.
That is what took you from Limbe's First Instance Court to
Bili.
I still remember that heady Okada Boy who hit your right
ankle.
That idiotic, unlicensed Achaba Boy almost killed an innocent
soul
With that mad speed of his on that crowded ENSAB Street.
He only hooted ONCE and marched in like the Russian Red
Army
At River Oder and Neisse, not tempering his deadly speed.
Unfortunately and fortunately for him, he hit Forcheh's
ankle.
If Mr. Forcheh was our Cameroonian Magistrates,
That matter's incidence would be longer than Egypt's Nile.
But, Forcheh ended this matter at an atom's length.
This is how and where Simon met Jesus!

There and then,
I learned that if the Law profession is practiced well,
It can be a multi-track highway to Heaven and sainthood.
I turned to pen and paper to sing Forcheh's fame.
I took the pen and pain to preach the Good News of Mr.
Forcheh.

And yet, I still have a big cry, Sir.
We need more Mr. Forchehs! We need more of you
In this mobile-constitution, miserable, richly-blessed
Fatherland.
We still need ninety nine of such Joshuas to cross our new
Jordans.
While I have the means, songs will join ink to sing this very
Gospel.
Thank destiny for removing Forcheh from the chalk-board
profession
To the Mohammed of Law. Barrister, you are a real model!

(This poem was first written in 2008 and wasn't published in
Chaining Freedom
*because it was too prosaic and lengthy. I edited it on 19 and 24
February 2015.)*

Disappointed Lover

My entire heart and soul
I surrendered to her like a foul.
Under heavy loads of conjugal sacrifices
I staggered for her just to meet with surprises.

Even when across the endless bodies of water
My soul for my 'Queen' never ceased to cater.
In sleepless nights I scanned ceilings for solutions
To her unsteady flows, unaware she made confusions.

Like a sympathetic he-goat I rushed home
To cure my ailing she-goat back at home
Just to learn she scattered all liquid seeds
I sowed on her soils—this just for her selfish needs.

And here I am; still reading the Psalms
That should become disappointment balms
To soothe the badly wounded and paining heart
I had auctioned to my wicked cunning 'Sweet Heart'.

(Mbankolo, 28 March 2015)

In times of death and in times of war, a writer's ink keeps flowing.

Nipped In The Bud
(*In Honour of Mr Chia Philip Yimeh*)

Chia Philip! You have been nipped in the bud.
A human tree that bustled with life few years ago
Now lies lifeless at Njinikom Hospital, face upwards,
Hands by sides, mouth sealed in white funeral garments
As if you never wore wedding garments when you
Took Odette to the altar a few years ago for vows now
forgotten.

On 20th Mays you shepherded us your kids to Belo
To file past grand stands to remember our porous unity
But today you slept eternally at Njinikom on a 20th May
As if kids had not come down to Belo. Why did you abandon
us
Your flock just when we need you most? Just when we are in
the cold,
The cold of underdevelopment and frustration, the cold of
your absence?

Dying at your age is life wasted, it is achievements dumped…

No more broad smiles on Langwa's face on Ango's verandas?
No more gentle steps treading Mbesa streets sharing love?
No more oratory at my book launches at Fon's Palace?
No more Ba Philippa at GSS Mbessa fathering me and
others?
No more elder brother and friend to advise and encourage
me?

Your sudden death caught me unawares
Like Jesus' took the twelve aback countless years ago.
The responsibilities you have heaped down on us
Are heavier than mercury, are heavier than our weight.

Shall we be able to raise the abandoned kids?
Shall we be able to tender the flocks on withering pastures?
Shall we be able to feed the lambs on saltless stables?
Shall we be able to gather the people your tenderness called
to you?
Shall we be able to breed another crowd-gathering person like
you?

We need your seeds of charm;
Let your seeds germinate in each of us
While the rains still linger around, so that in the dry season
dusts
We may still sprinkle your droplets of love, peace, charity,
selflessness.

(Mbankolo-Yaoundé, between 21 May and 12 June 2014)

Innocent Martyrs

(In Memory of little Favour Nsani)

December 22, 2014 was doomed
To swallow lives in ferocious flames,
But we left Yaoundé in hope of homing to Mbesa
Without knowing some will home to…

In Bamenda we took different directions,
Some through Oku and me through Belo,
All in the name of homing to Mbesa
Without knowing some will home to…

Then Ndop-Oku road repeated Tonga,
Producing mysterious flames to roast:
To roast car and luggage,
To roast car and passengers…

Then car driver disappeared into bushes,
Leaving kids and adults and luggage
At the cruel mercies of wild flames
To lose flesh and soul…

In this war-like consternation and confusion,
Innocent kids were martyred through harsh flames,
Burning into dark, dark, dark debris
And wasting away angelic beauties like little Favour's…

At Saint Agnes Parish cemetery and at Asuh,
Unidentified, dark and compressed ashes

Were laid down to the earth's insatiable belly
In lieu of charming Favour and others…

Tears, tears, tears, tears, tears,
Bitter tears, bitter tears, bitter tears, bitter tears,
To see one's baby swiftly pass from life through flames to
death,
To see one's super-beautiful baby buried as a heap of ash…

Tears, tears, tears, tears, tears,
Bitter tears, bitter tears, bitter tears, bitter tears,
To see one's sisters and brothers turned ugly in hot flames,
To see young, charming girls stroll with indelible burns,
twisted bodies…

(Mbankolo-Yaoundé, 12 June 2014)

Roasted Martyrs

(In Loving Memory of Little Favour Nsani and
Other Victims of the Babungo-Oku Road Accident
of Saturday 22 December 2013)

Note: *The poem above on this very subject almost got missing in my laptop that went bad. Then I crafted the one below before I could retrieve the former. I decided to publish both so readers can see how the writing process works; how hard it is to produce a scene or emotions at different times in exactly the same way. This too happened to the poem* "For My Love" I & II *published in* **Chaining Freedom**, *2012.)*

Our Yaoundé exodus was to take us home.
But, did any of us know their Red Sea would be fire?
Our Amour Mezam bus' snail-speed and chronic breakdowns
Acted emissaries of doom in our gloomy trip home.

A divine hand supernaturally separated us in Bamenda,
Taking me and my baby book (about Mbesa) through Belo,
And luring many other Mbesa children through Babungo and
Oku
Like butchers luring innocent bulls and rams to their
abattoirs.

Long after Babungo, abattoir emerged shrouded in mystical
flames;
Those furious flames suddenly vomited from nowhere to
their bus.
Their property was ravaged like wares in our ever-burning
markets,

Roasting little Favour and Langji's son to paradise as dark smoke.

Two innocent little human bodies reduced to meaty rubbles!
Light complexions like Favour's transformed into dark roasted corpses,
While adult survivors lost chunks of flesh on bellies, arms, backs, faces...
Roasted twisted arms, deformed burned faces, maladjusted roasted mouths...
Rivers of tears sprang up from families that happily waited newborns
And received two little coffins filled with two burnt little corpses.
Clouds of sadness shrouded families that held Xmas parties in hospitals!
Were they baptised in flames to resurrect in smoke into celestial bliss?

(Mbankolo, 10 March 2015)

To The Soldiers Up North
(For Cameroon's Defence Forces)

Hail national warriors up north!
We salute your bravery and sacrifices!
Hail defenders of our triangular frontiers!
We praise your loyalty to this Cradle of our Fathers!
We know like the Lamb you are wounded for our sake;
We know you are slaughtered for our safety;
We know you are bombed and suffocated for our peace.

Keep the faith like soldiers ants;
We march and pray every day for you.
Keep the courage like worker bees;
We sing and cheer every second for you.
Like soldier ants, attack and bite mindless of falling brothers!
Like soldier bees, sting and defend mindless of enemy
smokes!
In every village and city, we are gathering your food.

Send us your fallen brethren
And we shall resurrect them into our national pantheons.
Send us your injured brethren
And we shall dry their blood with our wetted handkerchiefs.
We find it needless to tell you this:
That not all the food and money we raise reach you;
That many thieves flood the resting king with glories of your
exploits.

Never mind the king's relaxation trips on foreign beaches;
Plus or minus the king, our kingdom must thrive on.
Never mind our drugged brothers fighting in the enemy's
camp;
When you catch them, we shall exorcise them for re-
integration.
We don't deem it necessary to inform you—
That the crown did not bless those burial mats with the royal
whisk;
That royal family went for feasts in unknown villages whilst
you were up.

Just finish the war up there first,
Before we perform the internal cleansing rites.
Just concentrate on the intruding enemies first,
Because we are already used to the enemies within.
Just focus on protecting our national compound first
Before we call the great family meeting
That will yield new family figure heads in this fertile family.

(Mbankolo, 27 March 2015)

Tribal Refugees
(Remembering Mbesa-Oku War in 2007)

In Mbesa:
Countless thunderous gunshots fill Mbesa air—
Poh! Poh! Poh! Poh! Poh! Poh! Poh!
Clouds of smoke from burning Mbesa houses
Spread darkness across Mbesa skies—
Smokes from misused matches in brothers' hands.

Burning pigs in sties and goats in pens
Mix with gunshots as they explode thunderously.

Burning Indian bamboos on thatched houses fire shots too:
Poh! Poh! Poh! Poh! Poh! Poh! Poh! Poh!

Behold our land-thirsty brothers maddened by land-thirst!
Pregnant women and nursing mothers,
Old men and old women,
School children and toddlers,
Women and men with children fastened on their backs,
Women and men pulling children along—
Burdened by heavy loads of rescued property—
Scatter in several directions like bomb victims in Syria—
Some to Akeh, others to Ajung and Achain;
Some to Din, others to Ijim and Kom...

In neighbouring villages:
These tribal refugees seek refuge in despair
Praying that Feyiyn and Yaoundé will save them

Return home and till their coveted, war-baked fertile
farmlands...

(Mbankolo, 28 March 2015)

Only an impotent writer can watch their culture depreciate like bathing soap.

But Today...

When we were toddlers,
Every nursing mother was a universal breast-feeder
On whose chest hung diverse babies suckling voraciously
Like calves at Ijim ranges with milk running down cheeks.
But today, infectious diseases have thwarted communal rules.

When we were toddlers,
Our babysitters ground our coco-yams in their mouths
Like grinding mills do with housewives' maize to feed
families.
Their saliva lubricated the chewed food to catapult us into
growth.
But today, migrant maladies have revised the unwritten rules.

When we were toddlers,
Our mothers roasted coco-yams and potatoes for us
At Adongtang[1] and Angem[2] fertile farmlands and forests
Where we galloped in fatigue to appease our stomach gods
And sip sparkling water from shiny gourds after hectic school
days.
But today, streams and springs have died from environmental
chaos.

When we were toddlers,
When calm and frog-croaking darkness covered the land,

---

[1] Farming region in Mbesa
[2] Farming region in Mbesa

We gathered round family fire places, roasting maize, cooking
food,
And telling stories to call home sleep and shorten the long
nights.
'Moaga'ana!' storyteller would say; 'shingo'ona!' audience
would respond.
But today, flat screened TV sets and Facebook have
kidnapped all youths.

When we were toddlers,
In moonlit and in glowing-faggot-lit nights, young boys
would go,
Making rounds of the village with entertainment like Hausa
drummers.
Koliko'o and Anyanga'a masquerades, followers, songs, beer-
cork rattles...
Breathed life and boom into lonely lifeless nights in our
virtuous villages.
But today, porno-music & vulgarity have conquered our
vicious towns.

(Mbankolo, 17 February 2015)

Those And These Are Our Names

They label, brand and commodify us;
Calling us blacks, niggards and Negroes,
Branding us sons and daughters of primitive cultures,
Christening us brutes and savages in waterless tropics,
Labelling us descendants of raw material reservoirs,
Naming us inhabitants of muddy, dusty, lightless countries,
Using foreign tags to identify our African bodies & realities,
Trade-marking us as residents of malnourished economies,
Designating us as perpetrators of human rights violations,
Referring to us as dull and uncreative black brutes,
Identifying us as rapists and abusers of demon-crazy...
For them, those are our names, our labels, and our
trademarks.

But for us, we are what we are; not what they fantasise about
us.
We each carry our names the way the nine planets carry
theirs.
We bear as many ethnic nationalities as the stars in the sky.
We own the cultures that have been sculpted into various
global cultures.
We possess the mines, oil wells and forests that impregnate
their economies.
We are victims of tourist-leaders dictating in Africa and
reposing on their beaches.
We are children of Kingdoms and Fondoms they forcefully
turned into Nations.

We own the forests and savannahs that green their smoky and crafty economies.

We are impoverished by ministers who enrich their banks with our resources.

We are sane humans resisting extreme and beastly human rights and freedoms.

We are children of evolving weavers and blacksmiths forced across sea shores.

We are brothers and sisters of the brains drained to engrain their faculties.

We are stubborn and unreceptive dustbins of far-fetched foreign demon-crazies.

We are children of planters and harvesters whose products prices they decide.

We are testing grounds of brand new diseases like Ebola and brothers...

For us, these are our names, our only bitter sweet real names.

(Mbankolo, 12 March 2015)

The African Family

In real Africa,
Family is large and communal.
Each person has
Countless mothers,
Numberless fathers,
Endless seas of brothers,
And infinite oceans of sisters.
And that's all!
We never have widows and widowers.
No bastards and orphans too.

In fake Africa,
Family is small and individual.
Each person has
One mother,
One father,
Some brothers,
And some sisters.
And that's all!
Then floods of widows, widowers, prostitutes...
Storms of bastards, orphans, street kids...too.

(Mbankolo, 04 September 2015)

Build Black Barriers

See them importing strange sex wrapped in aid ropes.
Let us build black barriers to fence our Africa.

I can scent putrefying odours of alien sexual practices
Blowing across the Atlantic and making Africa vomit.
Let us build black barriers to encapsulate our Africa.

See them breeding maggots of immorality for moral Africa.
Let us build black barriers to guard our sane cultures.

Let us mount moral mountains against their immoral insanity.
They are the cankerworm and we must be the divine Dove.

(Mbankolo, 25 April 2015)

When a writer burrows into society and religion, they must emerge with warnings.

Old And Young Vendors

Wrinkled-faced old mother vendors,
Taunted by scorching tropical suns and freezing rains,
Under avocado-, groundnuts- and tapioca- selling baskets,
Hustle up and down hilly roads, fending for themselves and
kids.
Gathered coins and notes vamoose into hardships' pockets...

Moon-headed old father vendors,
Afofoh-blackened tongues darting in and out of toothless
mouths,
Dangle and stumble with bags hanging on shoulders—
Tattered bags pregnant with assorted wares and banned
drugs—
Tread along crowded streets in search of meagre means of
survival.

Hunger-ridden kid vendors,
Dwarfed by heavy trays of chewable wares on sale,
Risking future ministerial and presidential souls on busy
streets—
Streets filled with unlicensed and washing-point[3]
chauffeurs—
Roam major roads and streets while their peers sing and learn
in classes.

---

[3] A place where vehicles are washed

Behold the forerunners of our distant emergence and close submergence!
(Monday, 23 February 2015)

Mourning In The Bars

Draped in tattered rags and poignant socks,
These men and women lament Cameroon's
Progressive loss of flavour in beer parlours.
Repulsive scents of sweat, nicotine and alcohol
Warm these miserable drunkards saving in beer banks.

On empty stomachs they drink to forget rising prices.
They drown mounting rents and bills in beer lakes in
stomachs.
They mourn Cameroon's steady ascension into hardships.
Their minds float in the affluence of Ahidjo's vanished days
And their bodies drown in the volcanic lakes of present days.

Why have teachers become skunk of the earth? They wonder.
Why are soldiers treated better than medics and teachers?
Will prices drop down after the fake war up north? They
ponder.
Will bosses' kids ever study and be treated here at home?
With armed human wolves all around, how else can they
mourn?

(Mbankolo, 27 April 2015)

Swamps Of Emergence

Lazy streams crawl slowly along our swamps
Like a serpent that has swallowed a mole rat.
Thick nauseating leach in the bellies of the streams
Glides endlessly over sleeping glass and plastic bottles.

Houses of the wretched of the earth sprout in the swamps,
With quiet rusting iron roofs smeared with dust and smoke,
Some big and some small, some in planks and some in bricks,
Releasing toxic refuse to nourish aquatic life in the streams.

These pigsty homes where underfed dogs wag tired tails
Stand still under roofs with old and new corrugated iron
sheets
Mixed immiscibly like the biblical old and new wine—
Sheets crammed indefatigably to housetops by rotting car-
tyres...

Tired lumps of old rubbish heaps sigh and collapse into
streams,
Opening smelly mouths filled with assorted domestic waste—
Clothes, plastics, empty cans and bottles, rotting meats and
vegetables—
Warning us of doom and gestating environmental time-
bombs.

These are the sparkling swamps of our submerging
emergence!
(Mbankolo, 07 March 2015)

Kfem[4] **Sellers**

My Queen Shallote and I went buying
In Mokolo
With faces twisted by hardships
In a country shrouded in price hikes.

Winding in and out of food counters
In Mokolo,
We saw women glued to low stools in a line
Like wheelchair disabled in a congregation.

These women with sun-baked rain-washed faces
In Mokolo
Were young and old and energetic and steadfast
In a market corroded by stubborn prices and misdoings.

Some with babies on backs and some alone
In Mokolo,
These women were kfem sellers and semi-manufacturers
On short stools behind kfem mortars in a long queue.

Tok tok tok tok, they pounded and pounded and pounded
In Mokolo,
Pounding kfem for their scanty customers;
Customers reduced by escalating price hikes and strange
diseases.

---

[4] Pounded cassava leaves used as vegetables

With pounding sticks gripped firmly in hands, these kfem sellers
In Mokolo
Were skilfully generating incessant sweet rhythms
That begged for lyrics that flow like the Menchum falls.

(Mbankolo, 18 March 2015)

World Market of Diseases

Follow me!
Let's go CHU Yaoundé,
Our World Market of Diseases:
Let's go and buy cholera
In broken toilet pipes vomiting watery faeces!
Let's go and buy malaria
In maggot-ridden stagnant waters!
Let's go and buy AIDS
In un-disinfected gloves in this chemical desert!
Let's go and buy madness
In bags of corruption and pride!

Follow me!
Let's go to CHU Yaoundé,
The arena of reversed values:
Let's go and cure doctors
Infected by endemic administrative negligence!
Let's go and vaccinate nurses
Gripped by poverty and rubbish.
Let's go and rescue pregnant women
Giving life on broken beds without mattresses & sheets!
Let's go and calm down workers
Striking to ameliorate their inhuman working conditions!

Do you see this hospital teaching centre?
This is the epicentre of our Submerging 2035 emergence!
This is our world market of diseases!
This is where patients cure doctors!

This is where patients contract more diseases!
This is where the culture of insalubrities is acquired!

(Translated from French version, Mbankolo, 20 June 2015)

In Search Of Safety

In Africa,
Ebola comes ravaging and dissolving
Humans into abysmal tombs;
Boko Haram vampires spit mortal grenades
And slaughter humans like cows;
Xenophobic brutes unleash furious flames,
Lynching and roasting victims...

In America,
Colour fanatics bury arms in clothes
And sneak into prayer halls to kill;
Demented police officers plug triggers
At stainless blacks;
Die-in-killing head-wrapped bombers
Force planes into deadly collisions...

In Europe,
Blood-mongering forehead worshippers
Send press-people into blood pools;
Linguistic affinities share daggers and bombs
Across brothers and sisters;
Boat-bound visaless bushfallers sink
Into oceanic dreamlands of abundance...

In Asia,
Angry rivers overpopulate banks
Into homes, rendering humans homeless;
Calm winds provoked by global immorality

Topple trees & homes and sweep off house roofs;
Striking earth emits vicious vibrations
That kill and bury humans in debris...

In the Middle East,
African housemaids are tortured
And sexually exploited like ancient slaves;
Strange diseases appear from nowhere
To hasten pilgrims' transition to paradise;
Stampedes during pious pilgrimages
Crush pilgrims into religious martyrs...

(Mbankolo, 20 June and 24 September 2015)

When I Go To Public Service

When I go to Public Service
And stand for hours on end
Waiting for those little information papers,
I praise the state for creating sterile ministerial websites.
I write mental motions of support for the bosses in air-
conditioned offices.

When I go to Public Service
And lack space to sit under these tents
To wait for information on 3-year-old files in same offices,
I thank the state for its digital-phobia in this tech age
I fantasise appreciation letters to drop in ministerial
suggestion boxes.

When I go to Public Service
And hear workers shouting at unpaid teachers
And grey-haired, jaw-shaking retirees in search of merited
pensions,
I laud the state for preaching insolence to ministerial
receptionists.
I venerate these bosses who precipitate the death of teachers
and retirees.

When I go to Public Service
And hear workers urging service seekers to dance
Because a 5-year-old file in same office has moved a step
ahead,
I memorise praise songs in honour of all inertia promoters.

I write mental poems to worship our bureaucracy lords and
goddesses.

When I go to Public Service
And see customs officers submit integration files before
training
While ENAM coats and military uniforms radiate respect to
workers,
I glorify the state for dressing teachers in clothes of disrespect
and
I commit to hide this state-organised discrimination against
teachers.

(Mbankolo, 27 March 2015)

Fallen Tree At Public Service

Walking for the Nth time into Public Service this morning,
I saw a fallen poor tree on a tent and began mighty mourning.
This palm-like tree has seen same persons countless times
Come and go, sit and stand under dirty tents, for no reason.
Then it sighed and sighed and sighed, complaining to stone
ears
Of Public Service personnel who compel users into tears and
fears.

When weary winds ran past last night, this tree trembled and
fell
Under the weight of its frustrations onto a tent to ring the
final bell
As a warning to Public Service personnel against bureaucracy
Because when Foyn B disappears we must embrace
democracy.
Even now, the poor tree's branches still on abandoned tent
sleep
As do the Public Service workers who on documents fall
asleep.
If you are wicked to humans, can you care for a fallen tree?
If you cannot treat files on time, can you bury a dead tree?
If you don't mind teachers and retirees, can you mind a tree?
If you are inhuman to humans, can you be human to a tree?
As I await my integration, I await the poor tree's burial.
When I return for same integration will I see same fallen tree?

(Mbankolo, 24 April 2015)

I Am An Aquatic Emissary

I am an aquatic emissary dispatched by water creatures
In Yaoundé, Douala, Limbe, Bamenda and Bertoua.
Our aquatic vision is ecological consternation and chaos.
And I'm out to preach the Good News of Prudence
Like Pentecostals preaching the Good News of Signs.

I must warn city dwellers to repent and refrain from
Dumping refuge and toxic waste into water bodies.
I must notify councils that most city toilets end in waters.
I must inform dozy Yaoundé fellows of broken bottles in
streams.
We are sick and tired of dumped human corpses and
foetuses.

When our aquatic medics visit upland forests for medicines
To cure our intoxicated young ones, they meet artificial
deserts
Created by the same humans who send toxic invaders to our
seas.
Enough of this ecological xenophobia against fish, frogs,
crabs...!
I urgently summon all humans to tables of ecological
diplomacy.

(Mbankolo, 27 April 2015)

Screens And Greens

Screens everywhere, everywhere screens.
Greens almost nowhere, almost nowhere greens.

Growing laptop screens, aging valley greens.
Growing desktop screens, aging plain greens.
Growing TV screens, aging urban greens.
Growing tabloid screens, aging plain greens.
Growing smartphone screens, aging plateau greens.
Growing online course screens, aging offline greens.

Screens everywhere, everywhere screens.
Greens almost nowhere, almost nowhere greens.

(Mbankolo, Ascension Thursday 14 May 2015)

A Zoom-In On Churches

Classical Churches:
They designate others as born again
And charge them for fake miracles
And prosperity-driven evangelisation.
They deaden healing powers of the Gospel,
But point to Job and Solomon before Jesus.
Very rare crusades, but salvation comes first.
They extort cash too and present Christ toothless.
First, second and third baskets ring in and out.
Which then is the surest path to the upper bliss?

Pentecostal Churches:
They designate others as dead churches
And charge them for disempowering Christ
 And inability to cast out and deliver instantly.
They blast catholic relics and orthodox statues,
But embark on selling stickers, banners, oils, waters...
They point only to Solomon and Hannah before Jesus.
Miracles top crusade flyers while salvation tails them.
Offerings, tithes, seeds and pledges reverberate all over.
Which then is the surest path to the upper bliss?

(Mbankolo, 26 April 2015)

Ascension Thursday

Snow-footed Lamb rises through sky cables
Into the home beyond to set our feast tables.

Wounded Lamb ascends into greatest glory
After toiling down here to end our gory.

Winged human creatures await Lamb in hope
Ready to offer Him for our sake a microscope.

From above, Lamb will scrutinise all worshippers
Selecting virtuous from vicious and false preachers.

Like a surgeon in a lab, Lamb will screen all prophets,
Blacklisting all wealth-preaching and fake prophets.

Lamb will be back soon, very soon, very soon,
To end this Gospel business, perhaps even before noon.

(Mbankolo, Ascension Thursday 14 May 2015)

Our physical political fields are too slippery; it is safer to start on paper fields.

Lessons From Naija Fondom

Naija villagers recently dethroned their old Fon
And they have peacefully enthroned a new Fon.
They each raised a single finger for chosen Fon
And foreign gadgets counted fingers for the Fon.

Our tired Fon quickly congratulated them.
Our sit-glued Fon tele-thanked their old & new Fons.
We hope our disgraced Fon saw the single raised fingers
there!
We hope he will improve finger raising-counting and retire
here!

(Mbankolo, 16 April 2015)

Museums In The Mind

Built indelibly on the rocks of my stubborn mind
Are museums for our neglected collective artefacts.
My mind stubbornly safeguards silenced and forgotten
Relics, statues, books, photos, videos & souvenirs of our past.
Posterity will never rub me with the excrements of their fury.

Kids marching past with effigies of Ahidjo, Foncha, Nyobe &
Jua.
Photos of Endeley, Ouandji, Galega I, Akwa, Fonlon, Beti,
and others.
Engraved in golden letters on their segment of the museum
is:
"Selfless Forefathers of our Independence, Never Power
Mongers".
Ahidjo's effigy and photos are threatened and shaken by
Southern winds!

Museum shelves pregnant with books and bibles of truth;
Books banned and banished like Rushdie's *The Satanic Verses*;
Books banned, burned and buried with their poisoned
authors
Like slaves buried to accompany master kings & queens in
the past.
These books and bibles are our collective memory; they are
our infinite CPUs.

Gingerly arranged photos and videos of patriotic youths
Butchered and murdered in their youthful bloom

For venting and vomiting hidden truths and challenging sycophants;
Young patriots poisoned slowly, brutally nipped at the buds like weeds
For daring to uncover boiling pots of lies and vain promises.

Tombstones, grave insignias and crosses, golden epitaphs...
For suffocating university students maimed and slaughtered
By uniformed human wolves while they clamoured for reforms.
But speaking Nchinda announced 'zero mort' in lieu of obituaries.
Did River Wouri feast on countless corpses after the 2008 baths?

Relics, effigies, headscarves, photos and videos of mothers of freedom
Deleted like pencil drawings from historical pages of the nation
By ingrates, zombies, buffoons, gluttons, cheats, embezzlers, misogynists...
Mighty and merciful mothers & queens wiped away like designs on dust
By sit-tight chiefs and Fons who disgusted their pleas for resignation.

Behold miniature statues of anti-corruption & anti-tribalism crusaders
Dumped into the abyss of oblivion by architects of regression!

Behold skulls and skeletons of brave national soldier-ants
Whose deaths were unannounced after the Kolofata-Fotokol
feasts!
No space for souvenirs of bastards, liars, dictators,
embezzlers...
(Mbankolo, February 15, 2015)

The New Bank Account

*(I acknowledge **The Journal of Cameroonian Writers** where this poem was first published in November 2015.)*

Since the outbreak of the northern conflict,
Many of the millions gathered down here
Have disappeared between Yaoundé and Maroua
Like the national wallet between Paris and New York.
Much of the donated food boils in personal pots
While our troops wrestle with hunger and invaders.

Thank God a new bank account has been created
To save, secure and swindle the donated millions!
We are waiting for a national pot for the donated food
'Cause the patriots up north are deafened by roaring
stomachs.
Were the billions that sent minsters to Kondengui not in
accounts?
Are there angels among potential demons to handle our
accounts?

(Mbankolo, 27 April 2015)

Republican Parasites

In this plantain Republic,
Human parasites and rubbish
Are scattered and spread everywhere
Like wild locusts on green fields.

While we chock in smelly vapours of rotting dirt,
These voracious human parasites are busy sucking
Our banana Republic to anaemic and epileptic levels.
There is no pity in Republican business!

Our national blood is sucked into endless parasitic intestines
As white-agbadaed and black-coated parasitic zombies parade
streets,
Preaching country love, exhibiting latest cars, spacious
mansions...
Lousily flattering the Boss, they secretly backbite and siphon.

These parasites sprinkle sandy dust on disappearing national
cakes
And spread political fog and clouds on eroding national hills
And press thirsty engine saws on whithering national baobabs
And handpick all fresh buds sprouting on quaking national
fields.

Land of gory! Land of parasites!
Thou of death and sorrow, our only bar.
Thine demotion, thine be hunger,

And deep embezzlement forever more.

(Mbankolo, February 15, 2015)

Our Landlords

My landlord's rents grow monthly like pregnancies.
Pregnancies for nine months, but rents for eternities.
Who cares to regulate galloping prices
When every stage is being set for eminent crises?

Our landlords' landlords increase citizenship bills
And in our motherland we live on soothing pills.
Petroleum and alcohol prices are wet-season tomatoes,
But we are baked by murderous rays of our fatherland's foes.

We are renting our country from born-lucky leaders.
We are their livestock and they are our breeders.
Mais, on va faire comment?

Our landlords belong to other landlords permanently
And we are tenants turning into liberators incessantly.
Mais, on va faire comme ça.

(Monday, 23 February 2015)

Since 2008

The metamorphosis occurred in 2008
When Mbeh defiled royal rotation system.
A few grains of enslaved accomplices applauded
'Coz of material gains and faulty sudden death speculations.

Since 2008, Mbeh wields wild power without abuses!
Sane customary vanguards he persistently accuses
For lifting lamps of truth to masses caged in artificial
darkness.
For such is reserved the freedom of incarceration starkness.

Yesterday's friends have turned today's fiery fiends
Secretly leaguing with long-bearded human butchers.
These beasts of Shekau pour bloody libations
In vain attempts to dethrone Mbeh and break the unwritten
truce.

Don't our people say it's easier to start war than to finish it?
Don't our people know it's easier to light fire than to quench
it?
Don't our people say it's easier to pour than to fetch water?
Don't our people know it's easier to enthrone than to
dethrone?

(Mbankolo, 07 March 2015)

Eulogy For Foyn B

One day, Foyn B must move beyond
And our grief must not be profound
'Cause his rusty reign has been too long
And our misery he is bent to prolong.

On that day we shall chant cheerful songs
And push off the wicked corpse with gongs.
Our children will recount futures stolen
When this future-thief shall have fallen.

May Foyn B's soul in sorrow repose eternally
As he butchered our dreams & destinies infinitely.
Termites, devour him like village cakes he devoured;
And wait for the dishonest elders & killers he favoured!

Farewell, fatally foolish Foyn!
Goodbye, ghastly greedy Goat!
Sail sorrowfully, secretive soul Seller!
Move on, mad and merciless Modifier!

(Mbankolo, 23 April 2015)

At The Burial Of Foyn B

When Foyn B will succumb to Death's call,
Heavy downpours of joy and merry on us will fall.
My frustrated kindred and I will attend his burial
In moods and clothing not fit for any decent burial.

Old Man and Old Woman:
Here we stand in tattered rags to bury you Foyn B.
Down there in the grave is your wicked, greedy corpse.
Why did you retire us without proper preparation, Foyn B?
No peace for your heartless servants and your cursed corpse.
Torn trousers and skirt down, smelly stool on coffin they
drop.

Two Dreamy Drunkards, Male and Female:
Here we stand worn out by alcohol to bury you Foyn B.
Down there in the grave is your wicked, greedy corpse.
Why did you drug us with alcohol to stay in power, Foyn B?
No peace for your cruel collaborators and your cursed
corpse.
Immiscible liquid of beer, whiskey & spirits on coffin they
pour.

Two Wounded Soldiers, Male and Female:
Here we stand with wounds from countless wars to bury you
Foyn B.
Down there in the grave is your wicked, greedy corpse.
Why did you fool us to kill our brothers and sisters for you,
Foyn B?

No peace for your blood-thirsty servants and your cursed corpse.
Knees down, smelly puss, urine and bullet shells on coffin they drop.

Two Accident Victims, Male and Female:
Here we stand on crutches and amputated arms to bury you Foyn B.
Down there in the grave is your wicked, greedy corpse.
Why did you siphon road funds and nurse potholes on roads, Foyn B?
No peace for your embezzling colleagues and your cursed corpse.
Worn out crutches, blood- & puss-stained bandages on coffin they pour.

Two Teenagers, Male and Female:
Here we stand—joblessness but ready to bury you Foyn B.
Down there in the grave is your wicked, greedy corpse.
Why did you steal our future and stifle our talents, Foyn B?
No peace for your merit-manipulators and your cursed corpse.
Falsified, assorted & cockroach-eaten certificates on coffin they drop.

Sour spittle and dark phlegm on coffin some will pour.
Accumulated poverty dirt from bodies on coffin others will sprinkle.
Dark greenish, slimy water from waterless areas on coffin some will pour.

Broken bottles, grenade shells and cutlasses on coffin others
will drop.
Unseasoned, half-raw food and worms on coffin some will
vomit.

When Foyn B will succumb to Death's call,
Heavy downpours of joy and merry on us will fall.
My frustrated kindred and I will attend his burial
In moods and clothing not fit for any decent burial.

(Mbankolo, 23 April 2015)

My Motion Of Support

I thank the King for a stay as long as the Nile.
I appreciate the King for hut schools without teachers.
I respect the King for coin-stained servants locked and
released.
I marvel at the King for wisdom displayed in stagnation.
I grovel at the King's feet for instilling spirit of motions.
I salute the King for using jeeps to insulate himself from
villagers.
I congratulate the King for his natural self-enthronement.
I honour the King for saving and serving outside the village.

On the day of reckoning, the big King shall question our
king:
Why did your children not study in the schools you created?
Why did you hold the turning axis of royalty on one spot?
How many heads did you roll and how much blood flowed?
How much wine did you divert away from royal calabashes?
For answers, will the King open boxes of motions of
support?

(Mbankolo, 26 April 2015)

I Don't Want To Be President

I don't want to be
President;
I just want to be
Resident:

But assured
That any Resident
Can become President;
That any President
Can become Resident.

I don't envy
Your Presidency;
I do admire
My Residency.

Like the village town crier,
My mission
Is to envision
Freedom for all and sundry
& to uproot all thorns on path to Presidency.

I don't want to be
President;
I just want to be
Resident:

But confident
That all Residents
Are embryo Presidents;
That all Presidents
Are egg-shell Residents.

(Bastos, 29 May 2015)

Breaking Brotherly Bonds

When our foster parents died,
Our half-brothers lured us into loose brotherly bonds.
That day, they wore sheep skins and spoke like
honeymooners.
"Two tongues, two books, two judges, two everything",
They sweet-talked into our ears, passing for real brothers.
In two brotherly blocks to live in union, we both agreed.

Ever since we formed the union,
Our half-brothers have dictated to us from fatherly towers.
Since then, they've put on wolf skins and speak like slave
masters.
"Their tongue, their book, their judge, their everything",
They now on us impose heartlessly, passing for our real
owners.
Our brotherly bonds have over heated; breaking point is here!

(Mbankolo, 16 May 2015)

When a writer travels abroad, their pen and paper never stay behind.

Scholarships For Africa

Some western scholarships help build our Africa.
As few as oases in deserts, such are our grain.
They treat us like kings and fortify our kingship skills,
But they remind us of our African kingdoms.

Some western scholarships help destroy our Africa.
As many as stars in skies, such are our drain.
They treat us like servants, strengthen our serving skills,
And lure us into servitude in their western/foreign kingdoms.

(Mbankolo, 25 April 2015)

Draining Cards

For countless years,
Green Card drains away our brains
Like hungry SONARA pipes draining our oils in Limbe.

For some time now,
Blue Card has begun sucking away our brains
Like mosquitoes sucking away our bloods at night.

Sooner than later,
Yellow Card may sprout to empty our brains
Like Cameroonians emptying beer and whiskey bottles.

In the short run,
Can African leaders invent Red Card to block our brains,
And quit seats, inflect salaries and level politico-professional
fields?

(Mbankolo, 16 May 2015)

African Housemaids Abroad

(For African Girls in Lebanon and Elsewhere)

Enticed with free flights, these girls left Africa.
With hearts droning with hope, they sailed abroad.
Like bees looking for nectar, they scattered out of Africa
To babysit Middle Eastern kids for money abroad.

Washing machines with blood-oozing hands in Lebanon.
They've been caught in a web of neo-enslavement abroad.
Seized passports, blocked from talking homeward in
Lebanon,
Some start selling sex to survive sourly abroad.

Some accused of child murder and sickness abroad
While their garments of innocence ask after them in Africa.
Some served crumbs and slimy overnight food abroad
While fresh oily plantains stress mothers' pots back in Africa.

(Mbankolo, 25 April 2015)

Golf Paradise

(In memory of African modern slaves in Kuwait and elsewhere)

Strolling down Yaoundé streets,
You see walls, poles, and rubbish dumps
Tainted with miracle- and job- posters,
Promising breakthroughs, healings and visas.
You think you're jobless and useless
And that Cameroon is hell on earth
While Golf emirates are paradise on earth.

You reach home and can't forget
The job visa for 350. 000FCFA
That will turn you *bushfaller* and breadwinner.
You distrust your nursing diploma
And grade one certificate and sell farms
To raise money and fall into greener bush.
You abandon corn sprouting in your backyard.

Within a month, your passport and full photo
Fly to slavery market in Kuwait and back.
Your home-tight agent hides it from you
Until five minutes to your flight at airport.
Once you check in under his pressure,
He disappears before you ask any questions.

Your plane soon takes off for paradise in Kuwait.
Your job contract is for slaves and animal workers,
But your home-bound agent has switched off his phone.
Did Judas stay near Jesus after the kiss? You wonder.

You land and slave agent takes you to stinking dorm.
Your masters pick you up next day into modern plantations
To sleep with cats & serpents; to iron for 20 hours & eat
once a day.

Your master starts asking your waters to quench sexual
thirsts.
You're insulted, beaten, starved, and stabbed
To do nastiest chores and assist Madam in bed too.
You can't find the paradise you left for again, only dead
maids.
You're jilted from house to house to dorm to prison
And finally flown back home with no money, no diploma, no
dignity.
You're back in the paradise you called hell before leaving!
(Mbankolo, 08 July 2015)

Ocean Cemeteries

Wandering migrants from fruitful Africa
Piled in ailing boats like sardine in tins
Sail through unappeased ocean waters
In search of greener pastures and safety
On foreign and sandy shores out there.

When unforgiving ocean waters—
Annoyed by rising global immorality
Heightened by unnatural sexuality—
Start jumping up and down in rebellion,
Poor boats begin reducing contents to appease.

Then human bodies are littered in ocean waters
For fish and crocodiles to bury in ocean cemeteries.
Rescuers stream in to gather dismembered corpses.
Some survivors head to barren but hospitable Athens
And others loiter along fruitful but hostile islands.

Behind them lie virgin gold mines inside fresh forests
With brothers and sisters torn apart by foreign bombs.
Before them are lined match-box buildings and museums
Built by African slaves and loaded with stolen African wealth.
But Africa is hell and Europe is Heaven. Isn't Satan black?

(Mbankolo, 04 September 2015)

Istanbul

Gentle hills and plains
Spread along interconnected seas
Like land patches wrapped between gigantic roots.

Busy tunnels, busy roads, busy seas, busy streets...
Crowded tunnels, crowded roads, crowded seas, crowded
streets...
Droning cars, droning ships, droning trains, droning mosque
speakers...

Ancient churches and ancient mosques, one city.
Ayasofia, Sultan Ahmet, Blue Mosque, Stephen's grave,
Galata Tower...
Islam and Christianity, Muslims and Christians, atheists and
pagans...

Tourists pour in and out and across like rice in thrashers.
Sigara içmez everywhere, but cigarette stumps everywhere.
Spacious air & sea ports, rotting slums & shanties, but hoş
geldiniz!

(Mbankolo, 16 May 2015)

Across The Shores

A flying bird I boarded across the shores,
My heart flooded with joy and hopes,
To devour books from white educational groves
And return to improve quality of our services and chores.

At Istanbul, far, far off from our black ancestral shores,
I began riding dreams back to Yaoundé and Mbesa towns
In search of my invisible but immortal African soul in towns
Where tadpoles and fish are roasted far from Kribi & Limbe
shores.

My infinite appetite for Cameroonian delicacies
Began overflowing the banks and valleys of measure.
This placed me under the weight of homecoming pressure
And exposed the hidden truths of foreign insufficiencies.

I was compelled to travel incessantly in my mind,
Physically consuming Turkish and Istanbul realities
And mentally enjoying Cameroonian and Yaoundé niceties.
Do I hear greener homes across the shores are easy to find?

(Mbankolo, 18 February 2015)

And I Turned It Down

It was ornamented in rosy diplomatic outfit,
That Ottoman offer which walked through Internet
To lure me and woo my country into more South-South
marriages
Where prospering husbands thrive while feeble black wives
suffocate.

The empty offer reached me in full glamour and lustre
Like that white-dressed succulent angelic bride
Who cannot stain white sheets with blood in the first erotic
game.
My shock & shame came in the morning, after the
honeymoon flight.

The thesis versus non-thesis confusion and frustration that
followed
Exposed the decaying ulcers hidden in that maggot-infested
nuptial meat.
In that frail union, haunted by my lost black glories and
hopes,
I felt the cold of lost liberties and the weight of neo-
enslavement.

Every minute on their soil showed me flagging and paling
walls
In my family home beckoning on me for repairs and new
foundations.

More trips between Avcilar and Fatih only shouted at my
heart
To turn down the offer, go home and mend our broken &
breaking pots.

Their letters urged me to bring about 100 US dollars
And I hearkened like Peter did to Jesus, no more, no less.
A week's expenses turned my pockets into overheated oases,
Nearly making me a beggar on foreign soil like those at
Briqueterie.

Three months under strange skies with no health insurance!
And you sing günaydıns to me (on dry pockets and) on
strange soils
As if I have no bonjours, goodmornings, and
etukelainmenas?
Yet with same course contents and even gaps? And I turned
it down.

(Mbankolo, 15 February 2015)

If You Must Fall Bush

(To the African Youth)

If you must fall bush,
It mustn't be a wild, wide and empty bush—
Wild, wide and empty like a wilderness;
It mustn't be a scanty bush without fresh shrubs—
Shrubs fresh enough to thicken our African shores;
It mustn't be an epicentre of idleness and unemployment—
Where you only learn to twist tongues and rap upon return;
It mustn't be a baby bush struggling to stand on its shaky
legs—
A baby bush younger and smaller than our home bushes.

Rather,
It should be a thick, fresh, green bush—
Green like green grasslands at Ijim in the wet season;
It should be a hospitable bush that respects/values other
bushes—
Not a barbaric bush where you seem to be from Mars or
Jupiter...

Otherwise,
Stay home and cut our forests into bushes;
Stay home and water our withering bushes;
Stay home and plant our deserts into bushes;
Stay home and chase them from raping our green bushes.

If you must travel abroad,

You mustn't be piled into ships and boats along illegal
routes—
You can't reach Spain across barbed gates or Greece across
Turkish waters;
You mustn't hide yourself among wares in cargo ships—
Don't transform into raw material stolen from our Africa;
You mustn't sell away family lands and property to raise
airfares—
You need them when you eventually return like the Prodigal
Son;
You mustn't stir dirt in the few springs of wealth behind
you—
You will drink from these same springs when you return
without tap pipes.

Rather,
You should procure your plane ticket and travel like a
business guru—
The gurus who enrich and impoverish our black economies;
You should sign an international hiring contract before flying
out—
And you will be respected there like Queen Elizabeth of their
England...

Otherwise,
Stay home and keep our streets as clean as streets abroad;
Stay home and lay the foundation for our African abroad;
Stay home and make our visa procedures as complex as
abroad;
Stay home and green the bushes of our native black abroad.

If you must study overseas,
You mustn't badmouth our universities to get admissions
overseas—
You'll soon know education is enmeshed in business and
politics;
You mustn't become a vent for vomiting African secrets
overseas—
Their scientific secrets are kept the way kangaroos keep off-
springs;
You mustn't choose the same courses we offer here for
studies overseas—
Only a fool goes to her neighbour and eats the same food she
has at home;
You mustn't wear stereotypical garments of inferiority while
overseas—
Let your brains collapse any racial barriers and crown you
their superior.

Rather,
Seek overseas studies only out of absolute necessity—
And settle for courses that cure our scientific blindness;
Let them know we are all academic gods and goddesses—
So that they can also consult our own academic chief
priests/priestesses...

Otherwise,
Stay home and join in cleansing our schools to be like those
overseas;
Stay home and clamour for introduction of new courses like
those overseas;

Stay home and uproot all unethical professors—make our
schools too overseas;
Stay home and become valued domestic alumni, not alumni
of schools overseas.

If you must work over there,
You mustn't pass through tourist visas and soil you talents—
Insist and be hired as an expatriate 'coz colour difference is
no weakness;
You mustn't choose destinations that measure talents on
complexion scales—
Talent scales should never have holes and broken springs of
racism;
You mustn't become hopeless sellers of watches on the
streets of Istanbul—
You make them undervalue and underrate our great Africa;
You mustn't become a nocturnal sex worker on the streets of
Paris—
Must we lose our oil, forest and virginity to them?

Rather,
You should select top jobs and showcase our skills and
talents out there—
You should use your talents & skills to grab foreign meat for
our African pots;
You should be requested to apply for jobs, not barbing and
garbage jobs over there—
You leave your farms and oil wells here to toil in firms and
toilets over there?...

Otherwise,
Stay home and design dragnets for our domestic dictators;
Stay home and decide the prices of our oils, timber and crops;
Stay home and dig roads to our enclave village-paradises;
Stay home and create the jobs you die for over there...

(Mbankolo, 27 March 2015)

From Bush To Bush

I hear you left our backyard bush
To travel for greener fields in their bush?
And why are you moving like a rabbit from bush to bush?
Come home! The dung of our suffering has greened our
bush.

I hear you abandoned our natural familiar bush
To create trails of prosperity in their artificial strange bush?
And why are you moving like a greedy cow from bush to
bush?
Come home! The sweat of our toiling has greened our bush.

I hear you blasted university studies in our bush
Without proper papers for new university courses in their
bush?
And why are you moving like a starved goat from bush to
bush?
Come home! New faculties and courses keep greening our
bush.

I hear you blasted hunting tasks in our virgin bush
To seek already hunted tasks in their disvirgined bush?
And why are you moving like a monkey from bush to bush?
Come home! Constant ancestral libations have greened our
bush.

I hear you waved goodbye to our mismanaged bush

Promising to bring back billions from their crises-austerity bush?
And why are you moving like a locust from bush to bush?
Come home! The deaths of the embezzlers have greened our bush.

(Mbankolo, 27 March 2015)

Are You A Bushfaller?

Are you a bushfaller?
And you say you went looking for greener pastures?
Were you a sheep to feed on grass?
If a sheep you were, couldn't you find green trees in our forests?
Couldn't you plant and tender healthy shrubs on our fertile soils?
Don't be the gardener who goes begging for cabbages from a carpenter.

Are you are bushfaller?
And you say you went to work and study in their bush?
Were you born a job seeker to seek from place to place?
If a job seeker you were, couldn't you create a job for you and others?
Couldn't you grow yams like Achebe's Okonkwo for your wealth?
Don't be the river tadpole that went begging for water from a hill beetle.

Are you a bushfaller?
And you say you went for smooth economic trails in their bush?
Were you a crippled rock badger to travel on already-created trails?
If a crippled rock badger you were, couldn't you seek family help?

Couldn't you tarry longer in family groves and mines and shrines?
Don't be the bat that goes begging for wings from an earth worm.

Are you a bushfaller?
And you say you fled our autocratic chief to their demon-crazic chiefdom?
Were you a coward to flee instead of confronting your adversary?
If a coward you were, couldn't you unite other cowards for power?
Couldn't you strategise and raise your finger in dethronement ceremonies?
Don't be the lion that goes seeking refuge and safety among feasting cats.

(Mbankolo, 27 March 2015)

I'm A Run-Away Bushfaller

I'm a run-away bushfaller.
I was hooked with a scholarship
Baited with a master's thesis offer
Into a salty academic sea with no thesis-plankton.
This sea was in Atatürk's land.

I'm a run-away bushfaller.
I was enticed with an educational opportunity
Decorated with bursary and insurance promises
To wait for months with neither stipends nor insurance.
This barren waiting was in Istanbul.

I'm a run-away bushfaller.
I was attracted by a distant greener academic bush.
Right in, I found no fallen mangoes and coconuts.
Right in, I noticed an academic drought and pale stems.
Then my soul started off for Ahidjo's land.

I'm a run-away bushfaller.
I recalled the juicy strawberries back in our bushes.
My academic throat itched for young grapes in our bushes.
Minus long queues and delays, I can find honey in our
bushes.
Then I retreated back to the academic groves of Yaoundé.

(Mbankolo, 28 March 2015)

Before I Fall Bush Again

Before I fall bush again,
I will hover over the chance and terrain
The way hawks scrutinise hens and chicks
Before landing to get their food.
We must heal our colonial and neo-colonial wounds.

Before I fall bush again,
I will tele-scrutinise the offer and opportunity
The way lizards study and calculate flies and insects
Before pouncing on them for their food.
We must recover all we lost in the colonial and neo-colonial
robberies.

Before I fall bush again,
I will pass the contract terms through black microscopes
The way surgeons and lab technicians study samples
Before settling down to work on their patients.
We must diagnose and treat our colonial and neo-colonial
ailments.

Before I fall bush again,
I will meticulously survey the travelling deal
The way hunters closely study animals
Before pulling the trigger at the game.
We must avoid and forecast our colonial & neo-colonial
naiveties.

(Mbankolo, 16 April 2015)

Hard work, Creativity and Perseverance are the Gateway to Success; but Pleasure is incomplete without some Reasonable Leisure.

The Success Code

If you must succeed,
You must toil
Like solder ants in rainy season;
You mustn't coil
Like a lazy snake without reason.

If you must succeed,
You must work
Like honey bees in their abode;
You mustn't work
Like lazy snails in their abode.

If you must succeed,
You must be serious
Like a patriotic solder at battlefield;
You mustn't be furious
Like a hopeless footballer in the field.

If you must succeed,
You must be creative
Like a committed and thoughtful artist;
You must be imitative
Like a casual and amateurish artist.
(Mbankolo, 20 June 2015)

Work and Leisure

Good work leads to good reward
Like good seeds and care lead to full harvest.
But, never forget some rest and leisure.
This brings reasonable pleasure.

Serious work & humility fetch good wages
Like serious studies & discipline fetch desired results.
But, never forget breaks for leisure.
This brings reasonable pleasure.

Work without leisure causes health decay
Like learning without play causes boredom.
So, never forget rest & play for leisure.
This brings reasonable pleasure.

Work without pauses hinders production
Like studies without play hinder education.
So, never forget fun & games for leisure.
This brings reasonable pleasure.

(Mbankolo, 20 June 2015)

Work and Technologies

(My gratitude to the Modern Research Studies journal which first published this poem in its September 2015 Volume 2. Issue 3.)

During the Industrial Revolution,
Machines helped Man
To improve and increase
Production.
Man didn't eclipse to be replaced
By machines.
But Man was always
Working and working and working
Endlessly like a waterfall:
Working to make new machines,
Working to repair existing machines,
Working to design novel models of machines
Working to maintain his superior status over machines.

Let's not fall prey to these new technologies.
Let's not be captured and misused by technologies.
We shouldn't become
Slaves to Facebook and Twitter...
Addicts to Youtube and Google...
Toys to computers and tabloids...

During the Digital Revolution,
Technologies must help Man
To improve and increase
Creativity.

Man mustn't withdraw to be replaced
By technologies.
But Man must always be
Working and working and working
Tirelessly like road-ants:
Working to make new technologies,
Working to repair existing technologies,
Working to design novel models of technologies,
Working to maintain his superior status over technologies.

The End!!!

Afterword

—Far-off pastures aren't that green.

If You Must Fall Bush brings the wide-ranging poetic voice of Nsah Mala to readers one more time as he explores themes ranging from the wanderlust syndrome of the twenty-first century to issues of corruption and the emasculation of African traditional values. Reading the collection is like delving into a treasure trough since each page brings to the limelight a new poem with a refreshing idea and manner of articulation that makes the collection even more thrilling.

If You Must Fall Bush is a critique of the ill-informed opinion of youths who feel that far-off lands are greener pastures. The poet takes time to explore the different traps that Africans fall into daily, some of which include acts of voluntary human trafficking like accepting to travel to Lebanon and Kuwait. These are places in which human rights abuses abound as individuals, mostly young women, are imprisoned and turned into domestic and sex slaves. At the end of the day, the theme of dream deferred is established because they are abused and sapped of their strength and dignity. In the end, they achieve nothing; yet others still fall in the same trap. In the midst of this, the poet sets parameters in the title poem "If You Must Fall Bush" since to him the African youth who must travel abroad should do so after an evaluation of the options. Travel should be embarked up with a sense of dignity; African youth should not be coped up in cargo ships like the raw material that western nations are still exploiting from Africa. Some of them take great risks in open boats leading to the atrocities that occur daily on the Mediterranean as migrants die like flies.

Bush is used in the collection as a metaphor as the poet takes the sense of the African bush or forest and extends it to the aspect of traveling abroad in search of a better life. When the African goes to the bush, they often return with nourishment so traveling abroad too is expected to yield the same fruits. Unfortunately, this is not often the case as people just rush off without thinking and they get trapped in terrible situations. If one must embark on such a journey, the poet cautions that they refrain from selling family lands because that will be the only thing to fall back on when they return like prodigal sons. To show that there is hardly any certainty of traveling abroad, the poet expresses this truth through animal imagery as people hop from bush to bush like rabbits or grasshoppers. There is a lot that can be achieved in the homeland. Therefore, instead of people going abroad to become sex workers or street hawkers, they should stay home and develop Africa.

The poet calls himself a runner-away bushfaller as he recounts his own experiences in Istanbul. He is granted a scholarship to study in Turkey, yet he does not like it there as his host university starts imposing a non-thesis Masters on him instead of the initial research Masters he applied for. Though Istanbul is such a lovely place, all Nsah Mala yearns for is the bounty and familiarity of home. He sees no reason why people should travel abroad to study courses that are already being offered in indigenous universities. Mala is a young Pan-Africanist and he advocates for Africans to stay and work for the development of Africa instead of being lured off by the prospects of a better life that ends in disappointment.

Apart from the portrayal of the bushfalling mania, Mala also concentrates on themes of corruption in his native Cameroon. He brings so much wit and satire to this group of poems as he paints a picture of the bureaucratic situation that holds Cameroon back and mars the prospects of emergence. Ironically, hypocrites still send motions of support to the government that does nothing to ameliorate the condition of its citizens. The president is described as a king who has crowned himself and rules his kingdom mostly from abroad. This witty usage reveals the stagnant political situation in Cameroon.

Some poems dwell on the emasculation of the African culture through the adoption of foreign values that are not beneficial to Africans. Some of the beautiful values that have been corroded include the extended family system that has been diminished to a pretentious nuclear family. The aspect of storytelling which fostered unity in the African family in the past is also eradicated with the advent of the television and this makes it difficult for young people to learn about their culture. This is lamentable since people cannot learn to be patriotic without understanding their culture.

Other poems focus on the health system that is chaotic as hospitals are rather places where people pick up diseases while doctors are inept. There is also focus on the difficulty of publication by Cameroonian authors because of the lack of publishing houses in the country since most local publishers prefer to publish textbooks that will sell in the national school system. The poet also pays homage through eulogies to the death of loved ones and acknowledges role models.

A two page review cannot do justice to Nsah Mala's *If You Must Fall Bush* because of the diverse themes that the poet explores. The poet shows cognizance of current world trends and the ills that young and naïve Africans fall into by opting to go abroad. He also casts his poetical radar upon the situation in his homeland Cameroon and criticizes the vices that are holding Cameroon back from emerging as a great nation. Nsah Mala is a young poet imbued with talent, one that we should all look out for.

Louisa Lum, PhD
University of Douala, 2015

About the Poet

Nsah Mala—also Kenneth Toah Nsah—is an emerging Cameroon-born teacher, writer, scholar and civic leader. He is the author of two poetry collections: *Chaining Freedom* (2012) and *Bites of Insanity* (2015). The former has been researched at ENS Yaoundé and is also included on the booklist for Cameroon Anglophone Literature (CAMLIT) at the University of Munich, Germany. His self-published books are *Mounting the Stairs of Challenge* (2011) and *Do You Know Mbesa?* (2013). With a BA in Bilingual Studies from the University of Yaoundé 1 and a DIPES 1 in Bilingual Letters from ENS Yaoundé, Nsah Mala currently teaches English and French and serves as research assistant to Professor Charles Ngiewih Teke. He has begun publishing papers in international refereed journals. He turned down a Turkish Government Scholarship in 2014 and was awarded the US Department of State E-Teacher Scholarship in 2015. He is also a Green Champion of the Young African Leaders Initiative Network.

Printed in the United States
By Bookmasters